IMAGES
of America

HALLETTSVILLE

ON THE COVER: Shown is a 1900s northwest view of the Lavaca County Courthouse and downtown courthouse square in Hallettsville, Texas. (Courtesy of the Friench Simpson Memorial Library.)

IMAGES
of America

HALLETTSVILLE

Holly Heinsohn

ARCADIA
PUBLISHING

Published by Arcadia Publishing
Charleston, South Carolina

Library of Congress Control Number: 2012950107

For all general information, please contact Arcadia Publishing:
Telephone 843-853-2070
Fax 843-853-0044
E-mail sales@arcadiapublishing.com
For customer service and orders:
Toll-Free 1-888-313-2665

Visit us on the Internet at www.arcadiapublishing.com

This work is dedicated to my husband, Richard Kropp, and our son, Braden, for their continued support of all my many adventures in history.

CONTENTS

ACKNOWLEDGMENTS

This book is the product of two and a half years of work on the behalf of many dedicated area historians who contributed information and time to this project. The photographs used in the book belong to the Friench Simpson Memorial Library's digital photograph collection of more than 4,000 scanned images. I wish to thank the library board and Brenda Lincke-Fisseler for her assistance in securing permission to use this wonderful historical photographic resource.

Janice Buegeler Saunders scanned all the images used and contributed detailed information on individual photographs. Contributors to the project include Dorothy Grafe Bujnoch, Brenda Lincke-Fisseler, Janice Buegeler Saunders, and Irene Polansky Szwarc, who are members of the Lavaca County Records Retention Volunteers. Richard Karl Kropp and Braden W. Heinsohn Kropp also researched historical information used in the book.

I would also like to thank my editors at Arcadia Publishing, Lauren Hummer and Laura Bruns, for the opportunity to work on the project. I am very fortunate to have such professional editors to help guide my book project.

INTRODUCTION

Hallettsville is the county seat of Lavaca County in the Claypan area of southeast central Texas, approximately 80 miles southeast of Austin. To the north of Lavaca County is Fayette County. Lavaca County is bounded by Colorado and Jackson Counties on the east, Victoria County on the south, and Dewitt and Gonzales Counties on the west. It is comprised of 971 square miles of flat to hilly terrain with elevations ranging from 150 to 350 feet above sea level. The Navidad River drains the eastern part of Lavaca County. The Lavaca River flows through the city of Hallettsville and drains the central and western parts of Lavaca County. Hallettsville is near the dividing line between the timber in the county and the prairie.

The Lavaca River was once described by Rene Robert Cavelier, Sieur de La Salle, as Riviere de Les Veches, or "Cow River," because of the buffalo in the area. The stream is intermittent because of its dependence on rainfall, and heavy rainfall can produce flooding as far upstream as Hallettsville. According to legend, Jean Laffite once scuttled the flagship of his fleet, the *Pride*, near the mouth of the river.

Capt. John Hallet was one of the first settlers in the area. Hallet received his land grant from Stephen F. Austin in 1831; he built a small log cabin on the east bank of the Lavaca River but soon returned to his former home in Goliad. His wife, Margaret, came from a prominent family in Virginia. When her family expressed concerns about the uncertainty of pioneer life, it is said she answered, "I'd rather be the head of a new generation in a new country than the tail-end of an old generation in an old state."

Margaret Hallet donated land for the townsite in 1836 after her husband's death and moved back to the small log cabin her husband had built. She carried some merchandise establishing a trading post and before long, there were other settlers living on both sides of the Lavaca River. The spelling of the town combined the name Hallet with the French word for town, *ville*: Halletsville. It was first spelled with just one *T* by surveyor Byrd Lockhart. In 1847, it was mentioned in the police court records with two *T*s, and this spelling was kept. Today, no one knows for sure if the town was named for John or his wife, Margaret.

After Texas became a state in 1846, Hallettsville and Petersburg competed for the county seat of the newly formed Lavaca County, with Hallettsville winning an election held in 1852. Allegations of election fraud continued until 1860. The courthouse that currently stands was built in 1897, replacing the one that was built in 1853, and it is listed in the National Register of Historic Places. Hallettsville owes its life and development to the county commissioners court. The town's conveniences surrounded the courthouse. Horses were tied to the chain fence, and public scales on the southwest side of the courthouse were used to weigh hides, cotton, corn, and other produce sold to merchants.

Following the Civil War, the land around Hallettsville was settled by Czechs and Germans, and the rest was settled by Americans, whom some said could make the soil produce the most goods. This influx of new settlers transformed Hallettsville from a trading post into an agricultural center.

Hallettsville suffered two major epidemics. The first yellow fever occurred in 1867, followed by smallpox. Yellow fever was so deadly and widespread that travel was restricted by guards that were placed on all roads leading in and out of town. Permits that were issued to enter town were limited to one hour.

One of the county's first private schools, the Alma Male and Female Institute, was founded in 1852. S.A. Benton opened the *Hallettsville Lone Star*, the first newspaper in Lavaca County, in 1860, but both closed with the onset of the Civil War. The newspaper the *Hallettsville Herald and Planter* was established in 1871, followed by Czech and German newspapers in the 1890s.

The first attempt to incorporate Hallettsville in 1860 failed, but on August 13, 1870, Hallettsville was incorporated by a special act of the legislature. John Buchanan was elected mayor, and James Ballard, the son of C.C. Ballard and Mary Jane Hallet, was elected secretary of Hallettsville.

As of 1875, Hallettsville was the only incorporated town in Lavaca County, with a population between 600 to 700 people. Later that year, the town lost its charter under the "special law" and reverted to general law provisions. In 1888, a reincorporation election was held and passed. Fritz Lindenberg was elected mayor, and Joseph Kahn, Volney Ellis, F.W. Neuhaus, and Friench Simpson were aldermen. W.P. Ballard became city marshal.

In 1887, the San Antonio & Aransas Pass Railway ran a branch of its railroad through Hallettsville, Lavaca County, Texas. The railroad provided a vital economic and social link to remote parts of Texas like Lavaca County. Lavaca County started to grow in population as the railroad afforded better access to outside markets and to development of the towns of Shiner and Yoakum. The new population was made up of German and Czech settlers. The railroad connected Lavaca County to the rest of the world. In 1870, its population was 13,641, and by 1880, the population had grown to 21,887 inhabitants. Sacred Heart Academy and a public school system were both founded in the 1880s. By 1892, Hallettsville had an electric plant and waterworks supplied from artesian wells.

On August 26, 1890, a fire burned a large portion of the block to the east of the courthouse. In response to this disaster, the Hallettsville Firemen's Association was organized at a meeting held on October 31 of that year.

In 1913, Hallettsville had approximately 1,300 residents, 13 different newspapers, 13 saloons, 13 churches, and an empty jail. Much of the economy was based on agriculture, including cattle, rice, corn, hay, fruit, and pecans. Today, the town is also the site of the Lavaca County Medical Center, Morgan's portable building plant, and the Pepsi Beverages Company. According to 2010 census data, Hallettsville's population is 2,550.

One

PIONEER DAYS

Petersburg, the first seat of Lavaca County after the county was organized in August of 1846, was located six miles southeast of Hallettsville on Farm Road 2616 on the east bank of the Lavaca River. This photograph is of the second county courthouse. The two-story structure served as the courthouse until 1852, when Hallettsville became the county seat.

A native of Virginia, pioneer Andrew Ponton came to Texas in 1829. He served as the last alcalde of Gonzales. Ponton was judge of Lavaca County from 1846 to 1848. He married Mary H. Berry in Gonzales in 1841. Ponton died on July 4, 1850, and is buried in the Old Gonzales Masonic Cemetery.

John Himes Livergood was born on September 10, 1815, in Columbia, Pennsylvania. He arrived in Texas in 1837 and settled in Lavaca County. Livergood served in campaigns against the Indians and the Mexican army. He was a member of the ill-fated Meir expedition that was captured by Mexicans, but he was lucky to survive. He served in what would become the Texas Rangers, in the Lone Star Guards, and the Texas State Troops. Livergood married Sarah Perkins, and served as the chief justice of Lavaca County from October 1850 to July 1852.

John McKinney was the seventh person to serve as sheriff of Lavaca County. He was elected to office on August 2, 1852. On July 3, 1852, Hiram Stewart Foley assaulted Sheriff McKinney with a knife with the intent to murder. A grand jury returned the indictment and, during the trial on the testimony of three eye-witnesses—A.W. Hicks, A.G. Andrews, and John Laughlin—Foley was found guilty. McKinney was reelected to office on August 7, 1854, and served until August 4, 1856.

Henry Jacob Braunig (1861–1945), a well-known local photographer, was one of the founding members of the Hallettsville Volunteer Fire Department. He served as the sixth chief of the department (1900–1903) and the eighth chief of the department (1906–1918).

The Turner Stagecoach Inn was built by Louis Turner in 1872. In 1947, J. Weingarten, Inc., purchased the property from Nolen's and operated a poultry processing plant there. When the Weingarten Building burned in 1997, portions of the massive stone and brick walls of the Turner Inn became visible. These were later removed, and the space leveled for a parking lot.

The Lay-Bozka "Wedding Cake House" was built from 1878 to 1882 for Dr. James E. Lay. The native stonewalls are 18 to 24 inches thick, and the wood used was cypress. It has a Mansard roof detailed with red and white shingles. It was purchased by Mayor M.I. Bozka and preserved and recorded as a Texas Historic Landmark.

Sam Aronsohn Dry Goods, Clothing, Boots, Shoes & Fancy Goods was located in this new building constructed in the late 1880s after a disastrous fire destroyed the wooden stores lining this block. The inscription at the top of the building reads "Isaac Samusch's Block 1888." Stankiewicz Jewelry Store is located in a wooden building east of the Aronsohn Building fronting on Second Street. Notice the muddy, rutted streets.

Sacred Heart parish complex consisted of, from the far left, the music hall, Sacred Heart Academy (with the barrel roof in the middle), and the church to the far right. The old cypress water tower is seen in the background.

Sacred Heart Catholic parish was originally a mission parish of St. Mary's, which is located four miles west of Hallettsville. The first church was built from 1873 to 1882 with stones hauled in by ox cart from Buckner's Creek near Muldoon by the then pastor, Fr. John Anthony Forest. This stone church opened its doors in August 1882. Following the construction of the church in 1882, the first school building (on the right) was completed in 1883, with a second building in 1893. The structure on the left served as the parish hall.

The back portion of the above photograph is the original rectory built in 1881. The front portion of the rectory was added on in 1899 when it was moved from the north side of the church to the south side. It was torn down in 1962 after a modern rectory was erected northeast of the church.

This image shows an 1884 street scene from the southeast corner of the courthouse square with Smothers Grocery on the corner of La Grange and Third Streets. The sign on the building reads "Groceries & Beer." The man standing under the Lone Star Beer sign is Louis Turner, who owned the Turner Stagecoach Inn.

The wooden building housing Smothers Grocery was on this lot east of the courthouse square on the corner of La Grange and Third Streets in the mid-1800s. After a fire that partially destroyed the old wooden building that was J.H. Appelt's General Mercantile Store, a new rock building was erected by William Appelt about 1889. The fire, originating in the Appelt Rock Building, almost destroyed the entire east side of the square.

The two-story building pictured was constructed in 1888 by Dr. E.M. Rabb. It housed an optician and jeweler, as well as a bakery, the *New Era* newspaper office, and a saddlery. A. Meyerhoff purchased the Rabb Building in 1905 and, in 1909, erected the new brick building, a showplace in its day, to house Meyerhoff Dry Goods. True Value Hardware Store now occupies this building.

On January 2, 1890, the Lavaca River, swollen from several days of rain, had risen to within 15 feet of the rails of the bridge. The *Don Milo* (Engine No. 56) came to a rough stop at the edge of the river. The weight of its cargo caused the train to plunge into the floodwaters below.

The *Don Milo* carried liquor as part of the cargo, which led to consumption by spectators. The consumption of alcohol only added to the problems with the crowd of people present at the train wreck. The liquor was being smuggled from another state into Mexico.

This hotel was one of the earliest. In 1854, John Harrell purchased this property for his hotel, the Harrell House. It was located on the southeast corner of the courthouse square at Third and La Grange Streets. The hotel passed through a succession of owners and names until 1868 when the Lindenberg family owned it, and it became known as the Lindenberg Hotel. It was later moved, and in 1900, the Neuhaus Building was erected on the hotel's former location.

═══ FIRST GRAND ═══

Firemen's Ball,

GIVEN BY THE

Halletsville Fire Association,

AT

❋ Elstner's ❋ Hall, ❋

Wednesday, *December 31st,* *1890.*

You are Cordially Invited.

Pictured is an 1890 dance ticket for the First Grand Firemen's Ball held on December 31 at Elstner's Hall. It was hosted by the Hallettsville Fire Association to benefit the volunteer fire department. The ball was the highlight of the social season.

Horse-drawn wagons transported all the equipment the photographers needed as they traveled from town to town. The wagons carried tents, poles, backdrops, and photography equipment. Pius Fey and Henry Jacob Braunig later established permanent studios in Cuero and Hallettsville, Texas.

The beautiful home of the Otto von Rosenberg family was a two-story structure with wide verandas and beautiful galleries. This photograph of the house was taken on February 15, 1895, when Hallettsville experienced a rare snowfall. On January 11, 1909, at 8 p.m., an alarm was sent from the residence of Otto von Rosenberg alerting firemen of a fire at the home. The Rosenberg house was completely destroyed along with most of its beautiful and costly contents. Only the stable, located behind the home, and remains of the chimney survived the fire.

The Opera House Saloon occupied the north half of the lower floor of the Opera House on the west side of the square. In this photograph, John Buss is first on the left, and H.J. Heye is believed to be fourth from the left (with the beard). The man with the stick is Oliver East.

SACRED-HEART-ACADEMY HALLETTSVILLE TEXAS

Sacred Heart Academy Music Hall was built in the late 1890s. It was bought by the parish in 1928. When it was demolished in 1936, some of the materials were used in building the parish hall. The statue of the Sacred Heart from the front of the building was used on the front of the church when it was remodeled in 1932.

H.H. Russell was born in Mississippi and came to Texas in 1851 and settled in Hallettsville. He was appointed county sheriff and later became the first county surveyor for Lavaca County. Russell built the fine home in this photograph where he and his wife had nine children. Russell also raised Jersey cattle on his farm.

Once Sacred Heart Catholic Church was built in Hallettsville, Rev. John A. Forest moved his residence to Hallettsville, and then St. Mary's became a mission parish of Sacred Heart, as did Brushy (now known as Yoakum), Yellow Bank (now known as Koerth), Mulberry (now known as Praha), Shiner, and Vox Populi (now known as Nada). By 1895, Hallettsville had electricity through most of the city, as evidenced by the electrical lines running in front of the church.

The image shows the "Great Snow" on February 14, 1895. From left to right in the picture are the homes of Mayor H.M. Tippett and Joseph Stanzel. The old river bridge ran along the west side of the mostly frozen Lavaca River.

The Hallettsville Opera House was designed by J. Riley Gordan and built by the McKnight Bros. in 1896 for Kahn & Stanzel. Cultural activities and school functions took place there. Law offices and dentists occupied the office space. The first floor contained businesses such as the Opera House Saloon, a cafe, drugstore, and butcher shop.

22

Nachrichten was a German weekly newspaper purchased in November 1900 by Richard Waltersdorf (seated at the desk) and his sister-in-law Mollie Wangeman. It was published in this building, located on the northwest corner of Third and Texana Streets.

The image at right shows the 1896 Hallettsville baseball team. Pictured from left to right are (first row) Bob Ragsdale, Adolph Lindenberg, and Eugene Blakeslee; (second row) Gene Ferris, John Speary, and Dr. Charlie Lea; (third row) Tom Denison, Ed Pesek, John Huchison, Guy Vollentine, and Stafford Woodridge.

John Rothschmitt (1863–1940), a native of Germany, operated a meat market for 30 years. Upon arriving in America, Rothschmitt worked in Cincinnati, then New Orleans, before settling in Hallettsville. The market was located on La Grange Street next to Elstner's Hall. Pictured outside the market are John and his wife, Susana (née Rohan), with their six children.

This is the First Holy Communion group in 1898 in front of the Sacred Heart Academy Boy's School. The priests pictured are pastor Fr. Louis Netardus (left) and assistant pastor Fr. Alphonse Mathis. On the far right is the organizational banner of the Catholic Knights, Saint John's Branch 564—the oldest fraternal organization in the parish.

This is a view of the city of Hallettsville facing south. In the foreground from the left are Fey and Braunig Photo Studio and the H.J. Heye Building. The buildings on the corner of Main and Third Street housed several businesses.

This view from the west side of the Lavaca County Courthouse shows the unpaved street with horse-drawn wagons, new automobiles, electricity lines, and poles. On the left side, the Opera House is visible, with the Meyerhoff Mercantile in the background to the right.

This image is a souvenir postcard of the dedication of the Lavaca County Courthouse by H.J.
Braunig. It was dedicated on July 4, 1899. Eugene T. Heiner served as architect and designed the
courthouse after the Allegheny County Courthouse in Pittsburgh, Pennsylvania.

Two

MODERN TIMES

This a c.1900 photograph of the Hallettsville Courthouse. Notice it is just before 10 a.m. and there are several two-horse wagons tied to the wooden fence while four gentlemen stand and sit on the stairs in front of the courthouse.

The Neuhaus Building was constructed on the southeast corner of the Lavaca County Courthouse Square. The structure was designed by builder and architect Henry Schurbohm. The work on the building began in April and was completed in mid-August 1900. The property was demolished in August 1972.

The two-story brick building and the two adjoining structures located to the right of it were erected by Fritz Neuhaus in 1900 on the southeast corner of the square facing Third Street. Many small businesses operated out of the Neuhaus Buildings; among them were Brom's Furniture & Jewelry, City Café, and Zavesky's Barber Shop. Pictured here, it is also known as the Neuhaus Block.

Pictured is a bird's-eye view of the southeast side of the courthouse. The Schwartz & Reichman Building in the foreground is a livery stable across from the Eckels Hotel.

Shown in this image is a 1905 Hallettsville city street scene of locals, a horse and buggy, and people in front of the Appelt Rock Building.

In 1893, construction of the Stankiewicz Building was begun, and in 1896, Andrew Stankiewicz opened his jewelry store where Hallettsville Hardware now stands. In 1914, the Stankiewicz Building was removed to make way for a new structure. A. Stankiewicz is on the left, and Frank Grafe Sr. is at the counter at the rear of the store. An unidentified man is on the right.

This c. 1905 photograph, taken from the courthouse, shows a southeast view of the city. In the foreground, from left to right, are the Appelt Rock Building, Elstner's Hall, and the Neuhaus Building. The long structure in the background is the Hallettsville Lumber Company; next to it is the New City Hotel (later Eckels Hotel). To the left of the hotel is the Methodist church, and to the right is Sacred Heart Catholic Church.

Henry J. Braunig (standing) enjoys a cigar with an unidentified man. Braunig was a well-known local photographer and founding member of the Hallettsville Volunteer Fire Department. He was the sixth chief from 1900 to 1903 and eighth chief from 1906 to 1918. This photograph was taken between 1878 and 1909.

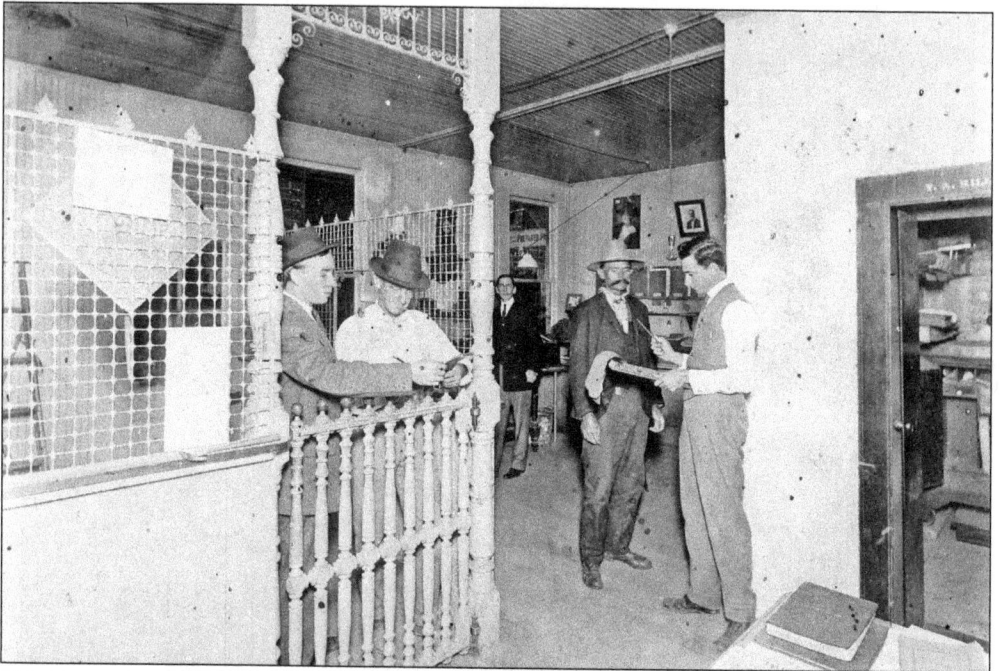

Shown is a view of the interior of the T.A. Hill Lumber Company. T.A. Hill's office is to the right. Behind the man in the dark jacket is a sign that probably reads "Prepared Parts." One of the notices posted in the left foreground just above the hammer lists rules for fire prevention. The building is now Hallettsville Lumber Company.

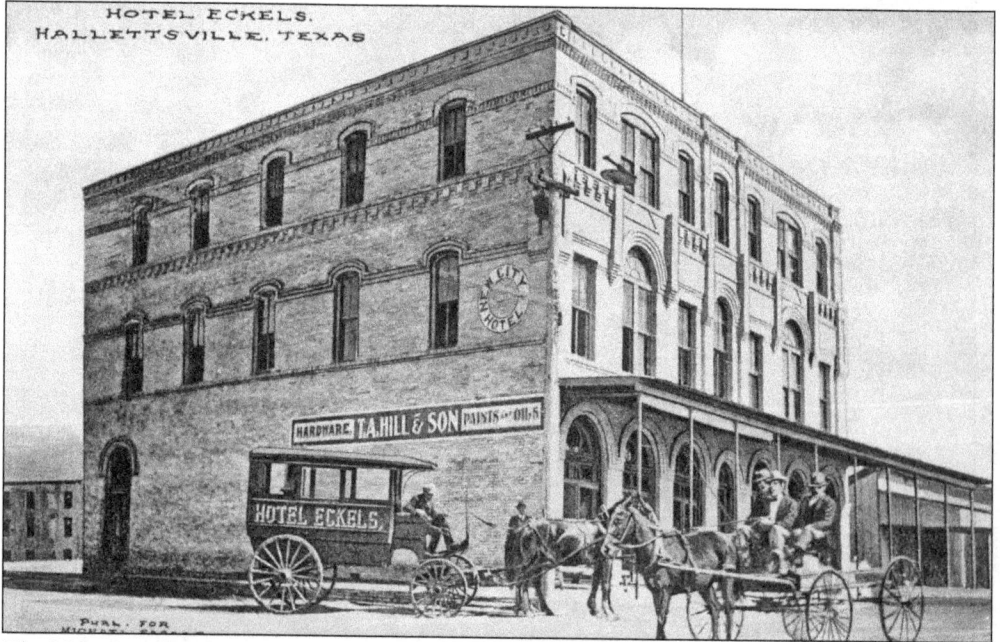

The New City Hotel was located on the southeast corner of Fourth and Texana Streets. In 1896, the Hallettsville Brick Hotel Co. built a modern brick hotel using part of the old Masonic Hall that originally stood at that location. In January 1906, New City Hotel became Hotel Eckels. The hotel was destroyed by fire in 1926.

This is a photograph of Nicodemus Morris, proprietor of Nicodemus Drug Store located on the west side of the square. His business was prosperous, selling large quantities of proprietary medicine that he called "St. Nicodemus remedies." These remedies were a collection of prescriptions from successful Texas physicians.

This 1909 photograph of two Czech men's fraternal organizations was taken in front of the Hermann Sohn Hall, built in 1906 and formerly known as the Schuetzen Hall that burned in November of 1901. The Hallettsville Schuetzen Verein Club was established in 1869.

On April 26, 1907, a trade excursion group from Houston, Texas, called the Houston Hustlers was greeted at the railroad depot by eight yoke of oxen pulling seven wagons that were linked together. The "Hallettsville street car system," as it was called, conveyed the visitors to the Lavaca County Courthouse Square for a meal to be served in the courthouse.

The Baptist congregation began worshiping together here around 1851. In 1882, land was purchased on East Second Street, and a frame structure for the sanctuary was completed in 1884. It served until the early 1940s, when the structure was moved to another site on the property so a new brick church could be built in 1948.

Since the roads were not paved until 1930, a water wagon, like the one pictured above, was used to clean the streets and settle the dust. In this case, the water wagon works on the west side of the square in front of the Opera House.

Pictured is a Hallettsville street scene in 1901 in front of the T.A. Hill Lumber Company, showing three unidentified local men with a horse. Horses continued to be an important source of transportation in rural communities.

In this local rural scene, three area farmers haul cotton by wagon to cotton gins in Hallettsville. The cotton was then transported by railroad from Hallettsville to compresses and sent to Texas markets like Houston and shipped to foreign ports.

The von Rosenberg stable was the only structure that survived the fire on January 11, 1909, that completely destroyed the von Rosenberg home and all of its contents.

NEW FINK HOTEL.
HALLETTSVILLE, TEXAS.

Mr. and Mrs. A. Finkelstein built the Fink Hotel in 1909 on the corner of Fifth and La Grange Streets where the current post office now stands. They had the reputation of never turning people away, regardless of their ability to pay. Immigrants were encouraged to seek them out if they were in the area.

In 1908, the Hallettsville Independent School District planned the construction of a new two-story redbrick school building that opened in 1910 and was called the "penitentiary." The building caught on fire on February 26, 1919, with a strong north wind fanning the fire. The school district utilized the old 1896 school structure, churches, and other buildings to hold classes on a temporary basis.

PUBLIC SCHOOL BUILDING, HALLETTSVILLE, TEXAS.

This is a view from the upper floor of the courthouse, looking due west at the city. The Opera House is seen on the left, with the old iron bridge into town directly behind it. From left to right, Charles Sentenberg Fancy Groceries is next to the Opera House, followed by the St. Nicodemus Drug Store, and then the Sheley Building.

In this 1910 photograph is county commissioner Eilers on the courthouse square as the oxen pull the road drag on Third Street. The road drag was used to keep the dirt roads smooth for travel. In 1930, the streets around the courthouse would be paved.

Frantisek Fabian founded a Czech language newspaper, *Obzor* ("Horizon"), in Hallettsville in 1891. *Obzor* ceased to exist in 1912. In 1898, the newspaper became the official organ of Czech men's fraternal organization Slovanské Podporující Jednoty Státu (SPJST) until 1912 with the establishment of the *Vestník* ("Herald") and Fabian as the editor.

Shown is a bird's-eye view of the Meyerhoff Building and the northwest area of town. Meyerhoff's was founded by Abe Meyerhoff and was built in 1909.

This photograph taken around 1910 is a street scene on the north side of the courthouse in Hallettsville with the Meyerhoff Dry Goods Building on the left top of the photograph. Next on the block is Kahanek & Renger Drugstore.

Meyerhoff Building, Hallettsville, Texas.

This is a picture of the Meyerhoff Building, located on the north side of the square on the corner of Main and Second Streets. Abe Meyerhoff purchased a two-story wooden building, constructed in 1905, from Dr. E.M. Rabb. Meyerhoff built the present building on the same location in 1909, which currently houses Rainosek's Hardware.

Hallettsville Volunteer Fire Department members pose in front of the courthouse on annual inspection day on May 22, 1911. Identified in the first row are, from left to right, A. Meyerhoff, Chief H.J. Braunig, assistant chief Richard Waltersdorf, Charles Pillar, W.J. Miller, Bert Riedel, W.D. Timm, Mauritz F. Nau, August Linhart, and John E. Buss.

Pictured here is rural route carrier William Harvey Turk Jr., who delivered mail by horse and buggy. He also served as postal clerk until he retired after World War II. Turk died on April 7, 1963, at 84 years of age.

The Hallettsville Hardware Store, owned by Scott Hill, was on the southeast corner of Texana and Third Streets. The store featured 70 feet of glass front and all of the most modern hardware in Texas.

Frantisek Jakubik began the Catholic newspaper *Nový Domov* ("New Home") in 1895. He died in 1904, and his wife took over the paper until 1906. She sold it to Joseph Kopecky, who remained the editor for the next 25 years. The paper was then sold to Richard and Joe Malec in 1931.

The H.J. Heye Saddler & Buggy Dealer float is in front of the Heye shop. Kneeling is a man identified only as Mr. Schubert, and on the float are, from left to right, P.L. "Pete" Netardus and Walter Heye. To the right of the float are, from left to right, J.G. "Griff" Traxler and H.J. Heye.

Pictured is the interior of the first Heye Building. From left to right are Pete Netardus, H.J. Heye, and Griff Traxler. Netardus worked for Heye for 13 years, while Traxler was a Heye employee for 21 years.

The Ideal Band was popular in the Hallettsville area around 1912. The band participated in the San Antonio Battle of Flowers contest for three consecutive years, winning two first-place honors and one second-place award. Members of the band included, from left to right, (first row) Casper Darilek, Ambrose Rother, leader Frank Rother, Paulie Rother, Ernest Schultz, and Ernest Lucke; (second row) Herman Schultz, Edmund Lucke, Charlie Rother, Julius Schultz, and George Schultz.

St. James Episcopal Church was established in 1876. Originally, members met in the Odd Fellows lodge until they purchased a lot on East Third Street and built a sanctuary in 1881. In 1913, the entry and bell tower were added. In 1962, the church was torn down, and a new church was built.

Pictured is the interior of the first Heye Building, which was a one-story structure fronting the Lavaca County Courthouse Square. Pictured from left to right are unidentified, employees P.L. Pete Netardus and Griff Traxler, and owner H.J. Heye.

This is the interior of the Traxler & Netardus buggy business, located in the Heye Building. H.J. Heye sold the business to P.L. (Pete) Netardus and J.G. (Griff) Traxler.

The photograph is of the newly completed Otto von Rosenberg house, now owned by Jesse Allen. The original home and all of its contents perished in a fire on January 11, 1909. Notice the child standing on the front porch.

In 1913, Emil Appelt built a new brick building on east Third Street. The post office moved to this new spot from its location facing the square on La Grange Street. Upstairs was M.A. Strunk's Rooming House; next door was Appelt Bros. Confectionery, and on the corner was the office for the German newspaper *Nachrichten*.

This is a c. 1914 south view of the city as seen from the courthouse. The double-arch building is part of the Neuhaus Building; next are H. J. Braunig Photography Studio and Stationery, H. J. Heye's Chevrolet, City Drug Store, and the Rosenberg Building. The road on the right is South Main Street.

This two-story brick building was constructed in 1914 on the south side of the Lavaca County Courthouse Square. Seated in front of the building are, from left to right, Griff Traxler, Anton Zaruba, Pete Netardus, Paulus Poch, H.J. Heye, a Mr. Bludau, Lewis Allen, Alfred Neumeyer Jr., and Walter H. Heye (standing). In the upstairs window is Lawyer McKinnon.

This courthouse photograph was taken sometime after 1914 but before the streets were paved in the 1930s. The public scale is seen in the foreground along with the perimeter fence and Confederate marker. The standpipe that served as the city water tower is seen in the background to the right of the courthouse.

EAT, DRINK
AND BE MERRY
IN HONOR OF
TEACHERS & TRUSTEES
HALLETTSVILLE LAVACA CO.
TEXAS SEPT 9 15

The Lavaca County Teachers Institute met September 6–10, 1915, on the grounds of the Hallettsville Public High School. The photograph is from a barbecue held in honor of the teachers and trustees of Lavaca County schools on Thursday, September 9, 1915, on the school campus.

Looking northwest from the courthouse in 1915. The Meyerhoff Building (lower right) houses Rainosek's True Value store. Across the street (left), the building houses the Masonic Hall on the second floor. Next, from left to right, are a warehouse building, Turner Stage Coach Inn, Orange Crush/Creamery, and the Lavaca County Jail. In the upper left is Rheinstrom & Greenebaum Sales Stables, built in 1905.

Fire Protection, Hallettsville, Texas.

Pictured here is the horse and fire wagon of the Hallettsville Fire Department on South La Grange Street in front of the fire hall. From left to right are Richard Waltersdorf, John E. Buss, O.T. East, and a horse named Headlight. The horse and wagon were sold in July 1920.

Henry Jacob Heye (1866–1957) was a well-known saddle and buggy dealer in Hallettsville. In 1916, he entered the automobile business. Among his many public endeavors, Heye helped organize the local Order of the Hermann Sons, the volunteer fire department, and the Rotary Club; he was also a charter member of the St. Peter Lutheran Church congregation.

Looking due west, the Opera House is seen on the left with the old iron bridge into town directly behind it. Charles Sentenberg Fancy Groceries is next to the Opera House and next is St. Nicodemus Drug Store. The two-story building on the right, the Sheley Building, was partially destroyed by fire in 1914.

The Theo A. Golsch oil well was christened in 1917. The man on the right is Alfred Appelt, and the well-dressed woman in the center and the men standing to the right are representatives of the drilling company.

The Civil War monument located on the southeast side of the Lavaca County Courthouse commemorates the Battle of Galveston (January 1, 1863) and was erected in honor of Confederate veterans from Hallettsville, Lavaca County, and surrounding areas, on the 50th anniversary in 1914.

This 1918 photograph shows the wooden graveside benches around the final resting place of August Heinsohn, located in the Hallettsville City Cemetery. Heinsohn, a native of Hallettsville and an early cotton ginner, died on December 19, 1918, during the influenza epidemic, reflecting one of the many deaths as result of the worldwide disease.

This military photograph of Henry Hruzek was taken while he was stationed at Camp Travis in San Antonio, Texas. Hruzek was a pharmacist and owned Hallettsville Pharmacy, later known as Hruzek's Pharmacy in Hallettsville. A grand opening for the remodeled pharmacy was held in November 1958. Hruzek and son Harry both worked as pharmacists. Hruzek died on June 1, 1972.

As late as 1930, more than half of the county's cropland was planted with cotton; however, because of the combined effects of the boll weevil and soil depletion, production of cotton had declined significantly. Cotton was ginned, baled, tested, and shipped to outside markets from Hallettsville via the local train depot.

Hallettsville's three Model T Ford fire trucks are on display on the south side of the Lavaca County Courthouse. From left to right are the 1920 chemical fire truck, 1918 fire truck, and 1920 pumper truck.

Photographed here around 1920, Katolicka Jednota Zen Texaskych (KJZT) Society No. 2, the Nativity of the Blessed Virgin Mary, is the Czech Catholic women's group of Hallettsville. Founded in 1897, the chaplain for the group in the 1920s was Fr. Alphonse Mathis, a pastor in Hallettsville from 1914 to 1938.

A Chevrolet car display is on the south side of the Lavaca County Courthouse Square in front of the H.J. Heye Building. H.J. Heye and Paulus Poch, both in suit and tie, stand to the left in the picture.

The Hallettsville Independent School District erected a new school building in 1920, and on February 8, 1921, the new school was dedicated. This photograph is the architectural drawing of the brick and stucco Spanish Colonial–style Hallettsville School.

The west side of the square, where the city hall annex is currently located, was originally the site of V.A. Hanak's watch repair and Sokol's Saloon, which shared the space. The above picture is of Hanak's watch repair shop. Pictured left to right are Otto Hanak Jr., Charles Zavesky, and Otto Hanak Sr. around 1921.

This photograph was taken looking southeast from the courthouse in 1921. In the foreground, from left to right, are the Appelt Rock Building, Elstner's Hall, and the Neuhaus Building. In the background, from left to right, are the Hallettsville Lumber Company, Eckels Hotel, Sacred Heart Parish social hall, and the church. Across the street from Eckels is the Ford garage.

Sacred Heart Academy (center building) was founded in 1882 under the direction of the Sisters of the Incarnate Word and Blessed Sacrament. The first school building was quickly outgrown, and a second three-story building was constructed in 1891. Shortly afterward, the two buildings were connected with a four-story, barrel-shaped dome over the middle. Two stories of porches

around three sides and a French, mansard-style roof were added. The music hall (far left) was built in the late 1890s. Sacred Heart Church, seen from the back, is on the right, and the society hall is on the far right. This photograph was taken on February 14, 1921.

Pictured in this 1924 photograph is O.T. East, who served as city marshal of Hallettsville. East was small in stature; however, he was highly respected by the town's people. Marshal East was known as "the Red Wasp" and usually had a cigar in his mouth.

In 1924, Henry Hruzek (left) bought out Dr. Boethel's Drug Store, which occupied the south half of the old Opera House on the west side of the square. In 1957, the upper floors were torn down, and the lower floor was completely remodeled. Hruzek's Drug Store remained in that location after the remodel.

This is a photograph of the reunion of Renger Hospital babies held on July 8, 1929. People in attendance included, from left to right, D.A. Paulas, Dr. Paul Renger, Dr. Kahn, and Dr. Boethel.

With the advent of the automobile, the face of Hallettsville changed. On the corner of Texana and Fourth Streets is a full-service Gulf filling station. In 1931, the finishing touches are being put on the new Hallettsville Tribune/Novy Domov Building (center). Next door, a Humble gas station is on the opposite side of the *Tribune*'s office.

In the foreground is the Magnolia Service Station, and next to the service station is the Heye-Zaruba Chevrolet dealership. Both buildings front West Fourth Street.

The *Novy Domov*, founded in 1892, was originally housed in the Sacred Heart Parish rectory. In 1931, it was sold to Walter Malec and his brother, who constructed a new, modern building on South Texana Street. In 1932, the Malec Publishing Company founded the *Lavaca County Tribune*, and the two papers shared presses.

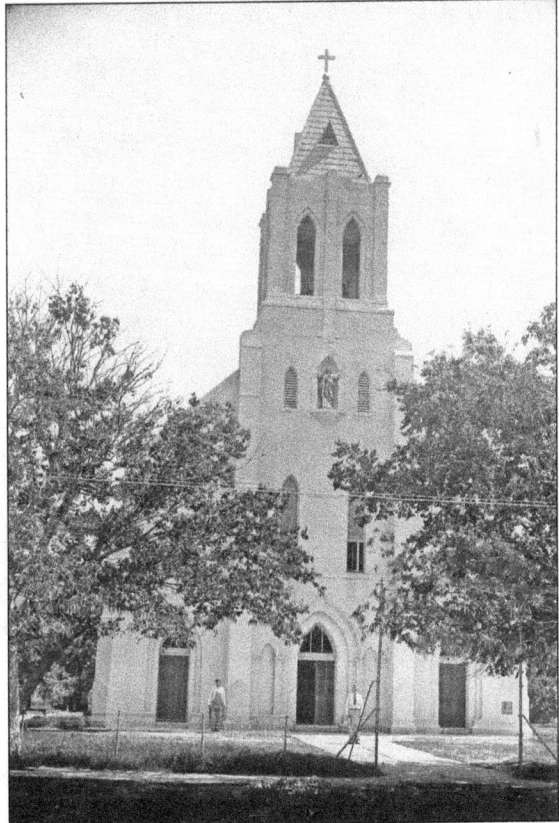

In 1932, Sacred Heart Church underwent an extensive remodel: a sacristy was added, the church was extended in length, the walls were repaired and covered in stucco, and the belfry design was changed. The statue of the Sacred Heart was taken from the music hall and placed at the front of the church.

Pictured is German-born Otto Goedecke, an American cotton merchant. In 1932, Goedecke established his business headquarters in Hallettsville, paving the way for modern methods of marketing and researching cotton. Goedecke was a merchant of cotton and the president of his firm, whose headquarters was located in Hallettsville. Considered a pioneer in marketing and research, he began the modern merchandising of cotton through scientific methods that are still used today. Goedecke incorporated his business in Texas in 1946 after beginning as a proprietorship in 1932.

The lineup for the 1933 football team was (ends) Elroy Coldeway, Yeager Reaves, and Maurice Jahn; (tackles) Hascal Gregory, Edwin Hollub, and Douglas Borders; (guards) Vaclav Kubena and Edwin Chovanetz; (center) Fred Strauss; (quarterback) Sonny Sommers; (backs) Dan Fertsch, Grady Whitley, and Bill Turk; (coach) Bill Eilers, and unidentified managers. They are pictured in front of a school building.

Here, the same players on the 1933 football team pose on the Hallettsville football field.

The Reconstruction Finance Corporation was an agency established and chartered by the US Congress to provide aid to state and local governments and loans to various businesses. The men employed in this program did a variety of work, including the drainage work documented in this photograph.

Pictured here, KJZT Society No. 2, the Nativity of the Blessed Virgin Mary, Hallettsville, organized in 1897. This Czech Catholic women's group photograph is from April 28, 1935.

Pictured here is the Hallettsville graduating class of 1926. From left to right are (first row) Lester Ziegler, Ervin Kubicek, Oscar Rosenauer, George Kahanek, Roscoe Thomas, and Robert Kresta; (second row) Alfred Neumeyer, Yeager Reeves, Nelson Copp, C. J. Hudgeons, Robert Pesek, Raymond Cheney, Wayne Terry, and James Garner; (third row) Pauline Henneke, Elizabeth Schubert, Luella Jalufka, Mary Stavinoha, Marjorie Janacek, Shellye Moore, Janet Rother, Cora Lee Terry, and Della M. Sommerlotte; (fourth row) Arthur McElroy, Max Berger, Elroy Coldaway, James Nance, Mr. Holloway (a sponsor), William Allen, Dan Fritsch, Raymond Eissler, and Charles Fitch.

The Idle Hour club, a black dance hall, was located at the corner of East Second and North Texana Streets. The property was bought out, and the club was moved a new location on Front Street.

The Lavaca River rose out of its banks, flooding the downtown business district in the early morning hours of Sunday, June 30, 1940. Most bridges in Lavaca County were either damaged or destroyed by the flood.

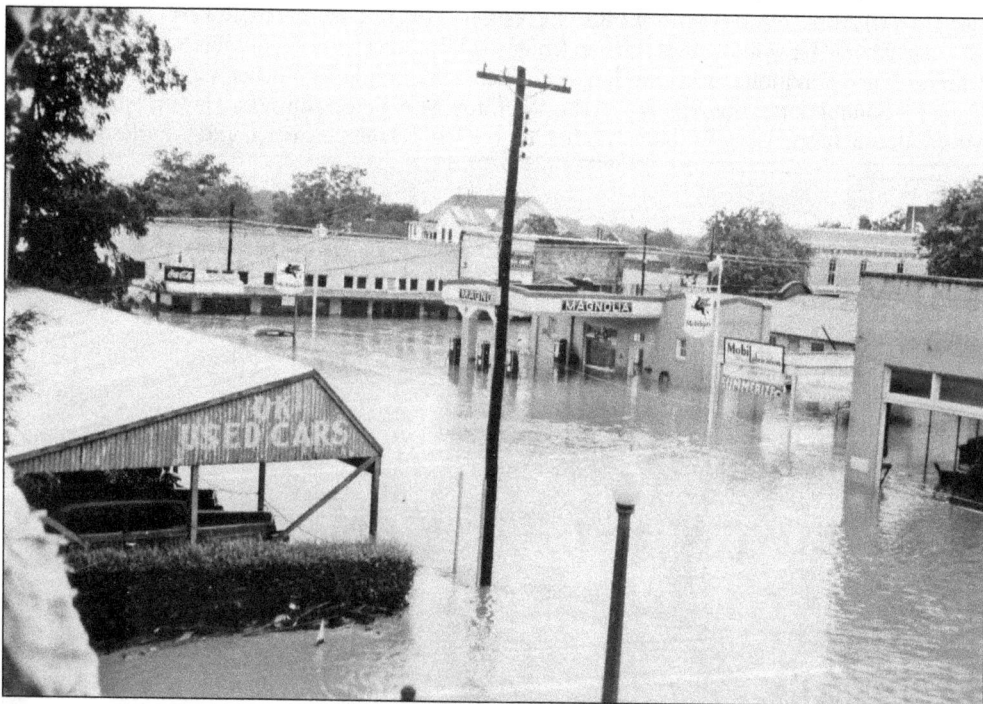

Seen here is a view of businesses underwater on Fourth Street. The Heye Chevrolet car dealership, Magnolia Service Station, and the OK Used Car lot are submerged. The flooding peaked at 9:00 a.m. that Sunday, and by 3:00 p.m., the floodwaters had receded from the square.

Pictured here is a view of the flood from the east side of the square, looking south down La Grange Street. Grant Lumber Company is in the far background.

This is another view of the flood on La Grange Street, looking north toward the square. Merchants lost about 85 percent of their goods at an estimated value of around $150,000.

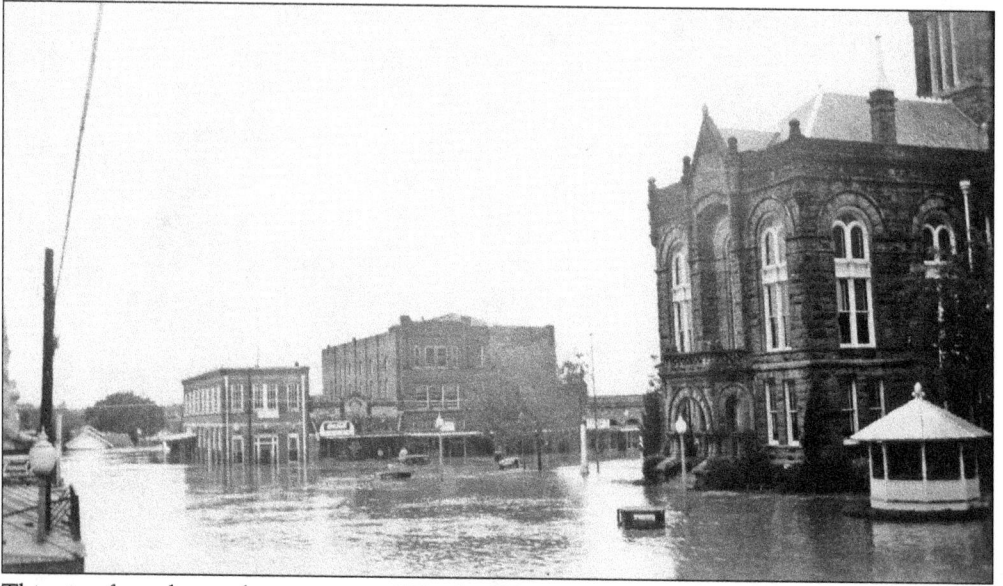

This view from the northwest corner of Third and La Grange Streets looks toward the courthouse and the Opera House. Cars are submerged almost to their roofs. Water is in the basement of the courthouse and halfway up the stairs to the first floor.

The First National Bank was one of the businesses inundated with floodwaters. Pictured are J.H. Simpson (right) Sr. and Bruno Cohn carrying records and water-soaked currency from the bank vault. The Lavaca River rose 41 feet—10 feet above the previous record—and became a raging river, taking seven lives and causing enormous property damage. Water stood 6 to 10 feet deep on the square, and as it receded, it left a layer of slimy mud on everything it had covered.

Three

DISASTERS, PROGRESS, AND GOOD TIMES

The courthouse square is shown during the flood. Notice the partially submerged vehicles in front of Elkin's 5-10 & 25¢ Store. Other businesses on this side of the square include H.J. Braunig Photography, City Café, and the Red & White Grocery in 1940.

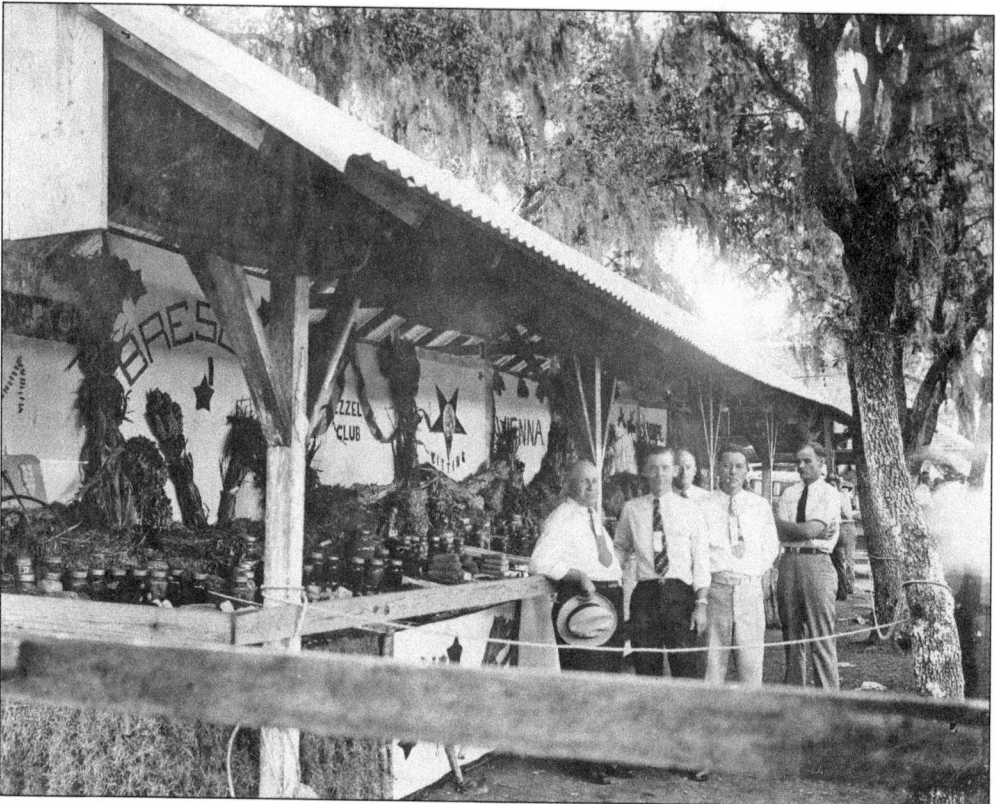

A fair held at the city park included canning entries from the communities of Breslau, Ezzell, Witting, and Vienna.

Pictured is a new fire truck purchased by the volunteer fire department from Burke & Sims of San Antonio in December 1940. The man on the right is Gus J. Strauss Sr.

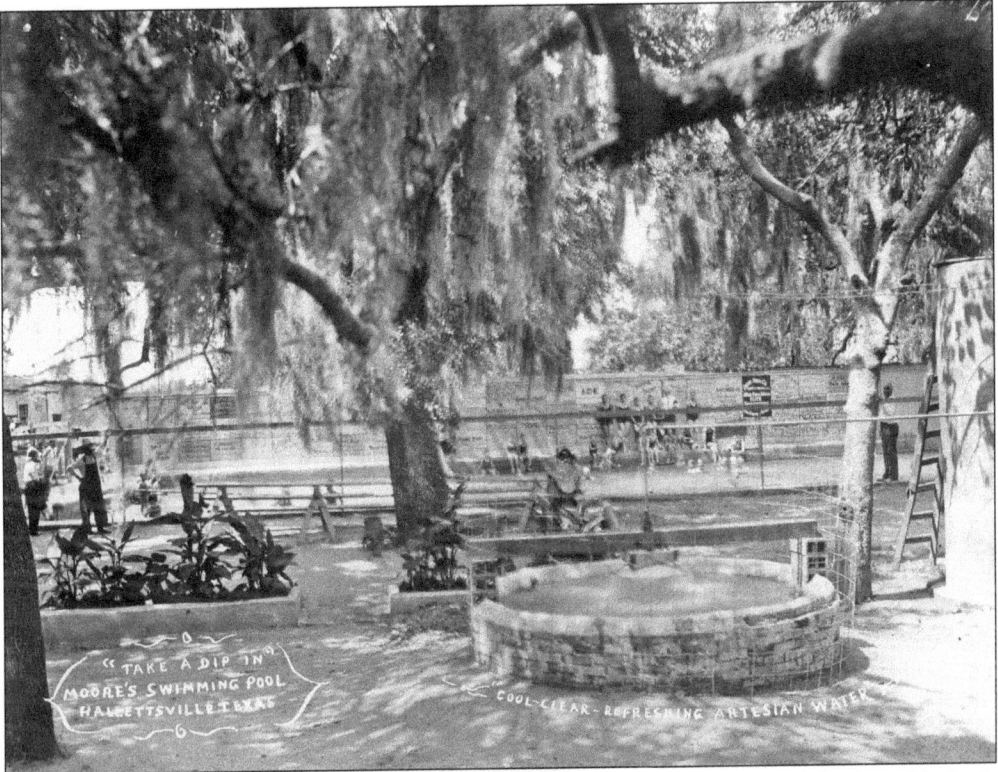

Hallettsville native Amos Vincent Carter Moore, a local contractor, built a pool near the public high school on what is now Judy Street near Rickaway Branch. The pool was fed by an artesian well.

This is another view of the artesian well–fed pool built by Amos Vincent Carter Moore. In 1941, Moore erected a sawmill near the swimming pool to cut shiplap, shingles, and hard oak flooring.

Moore owned and operated the local swimming pool, which was fed by an artesian well. He kept an alligator at the pool as a pet, and local stories persist that he would swim with the alligator when the pool was closed to the public.

The First Methodist Church of Hallettsville traces its origin to 1851, when it was established by 11 charter members. This photograph shows the new expansion that was added to the rear of the building in 1941.

With the advent of cars, more people were able to travel to town and to church. Sacred Heart Church, seen here in about 1945, was not prepared and had little space to park these mechanical horses. Cars would park on the streets for several blocks around the church.

Pictured is a back-to-school float from the second annual La Vaca Fiesta, held September 6 and 7 in 1946. On the float are Sacred Heart cheerleaders Mary Elizabeth (Bucek) Joinetz (left) and Marionell (Hemmi) Smothers. The float took third place.

The second-place winner in the Rodeo Kiddie Parade was the Cole Theater float. The children pretending to film a cowboy movie are, from left to right, Billie Fehrenkamp, Don Minear, Gussie Strauss and Bonnie Sue Morton.

Pictured are buyers and sellers at Hallettsville Auction Ring in 1942 or 1943. The auction ring seating reflects the segregation of people during this time period. A new auction ring was built in 1946 after the 1940 flood.

Pictured is the cover from the program for the first State Championship High School Rodeo held in Hallettsville on June 20–22, 1947.

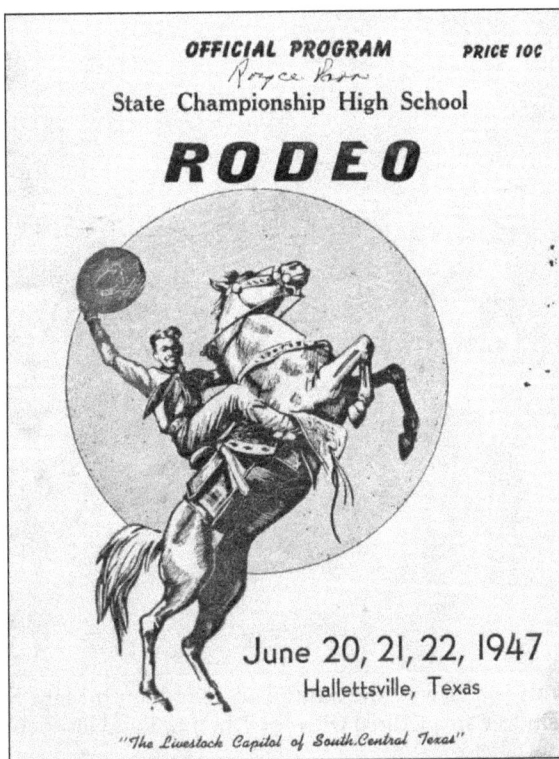

OFFICIAL PROGRAM   PRICE 10C

Royce Parr

State Championship High School

RODEO

June 20, 21, 22, 1947

Hallettsville, Texas

"The Livestock Capitol of South Central Texas"

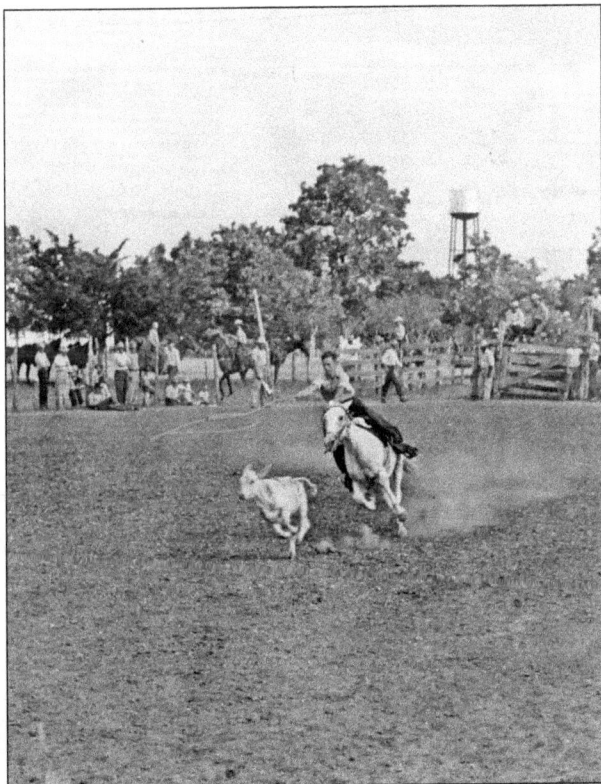

Royce Parr participates in the calf-roping contest at the first State Championship High School Rodeo.

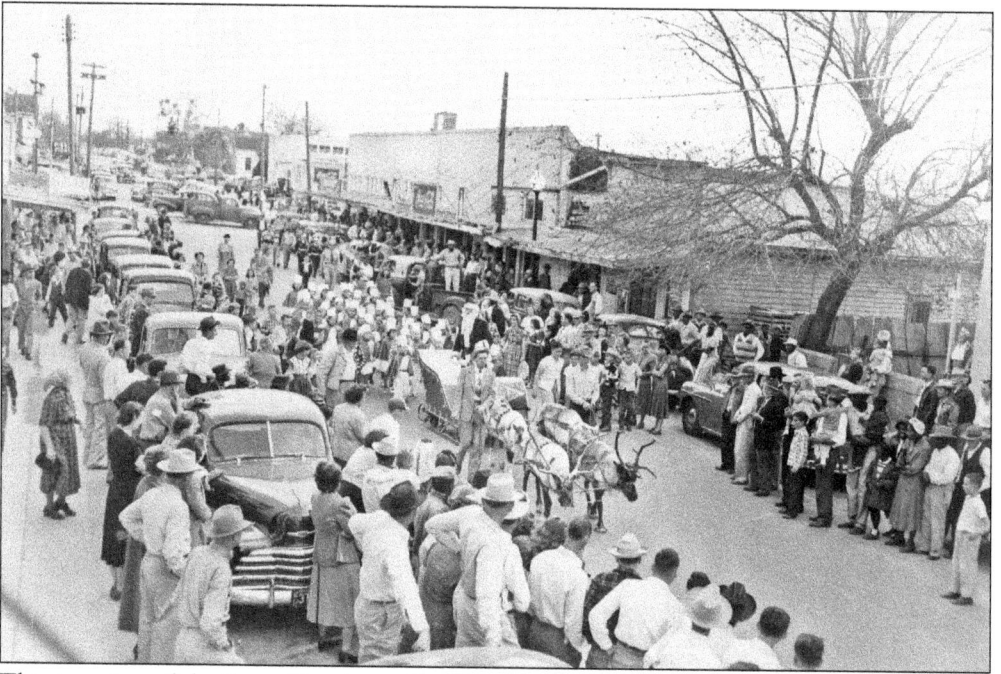

This is a view of the Santa Parade on South Main Street in December 1948. Santa's sled and reindeer are pictured with the Rhythm Band just behind them.

Vehicles travel in both directions around the Lavaca County Courthouse Square on North Main Street. The house in the background was the Seth S. Thigpen family home.

Started by Dr. Paul Renger in 1917, Renger Hospital was located on South Main Street. This house served not only as the hospital, but also as the Renger family residence. Construction for the new hospital began in 1949, and this building was demolished shortly after this photograph was taken.

Riders taking part in the June Rodeo Parade pictured include Leon Kahanek, Alton Allen, and Claude Mullins. All three men were lifetime advisory directors for the National High School Rodeo Association.

Known as the Fink Hotel for 43 years, it was purchased by Mr. and Mrs. Hugh B. Lyons in 1946 and renamed the Lyons Hotel. It was refinished and redecorated, and a new cooling system was installed. The hotel closed in 1959 and was torn down to make way for the current post office.

This view looks northward toward the courthouse square up La Grange Street. The Lyons Hotel and fire station are on the left, and the courthouse tower is seen looming over all.

The five-inch snowfall of January 1949 turned Hallettsville into a winter wonderland. Seen here is a view of the low-water bridge, showing the blanket of snow covering the river and the Hallettsville area.

Pictured is the low water bridge over the Lavaca River on Second Street. From left to right are Naomi Minear, Margaret Franta, Molly Strauss, Don Minear, and Ludwig Pete Steinberg.

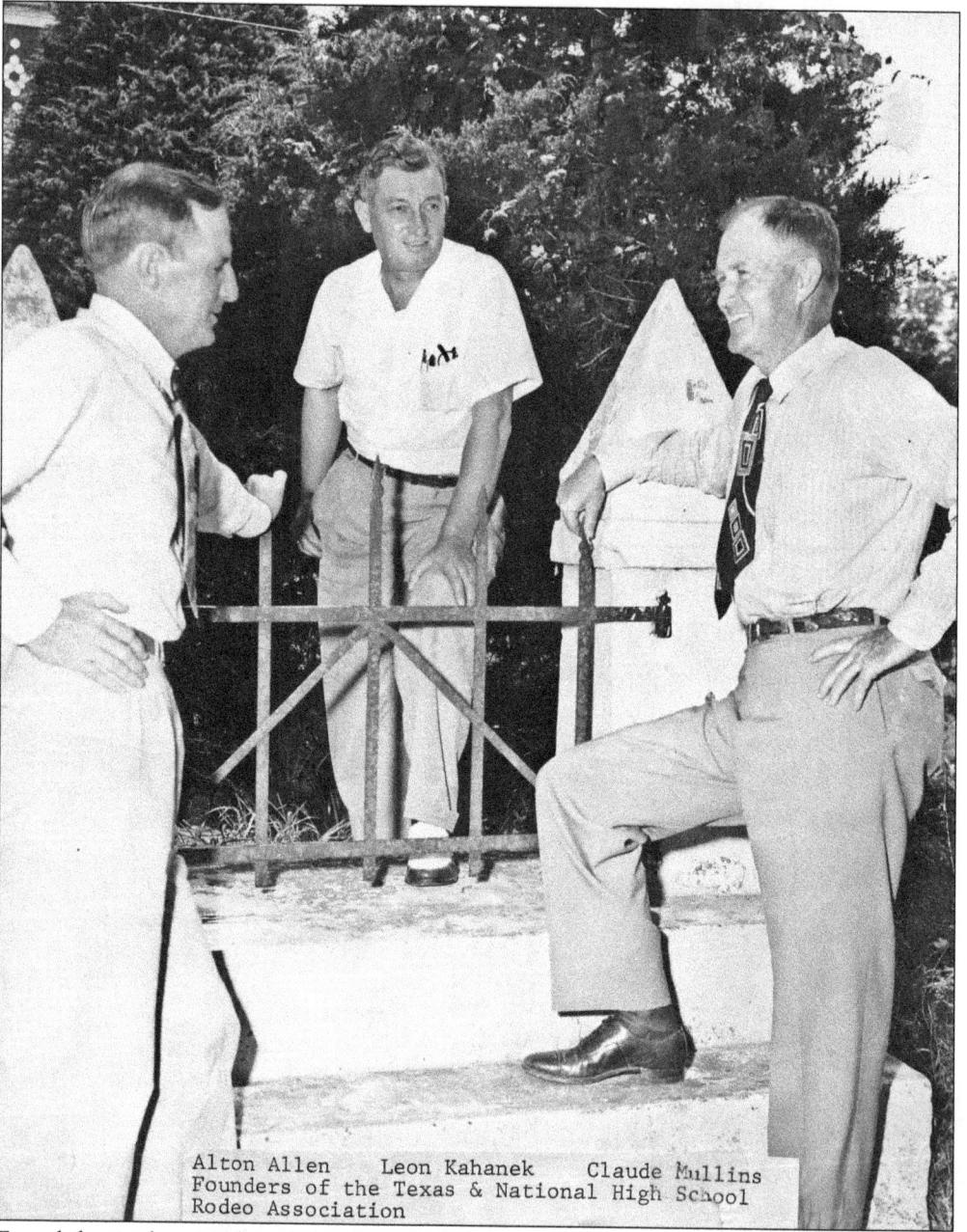

Alton Allen   Leon Kahanek   Claude Mullins
Founders of the Texas & National High School
Rodeo Association

From left to right are Alton Allen, Leon L. Kahanek, and Claude Mullins, the founders of the first annual Texas State Championship High School Rodeo held in Hallettsville in 1947. They went on to organize the first annual National Championship High School Rodeo, which was also held in Hallettsville.

ENTRANCE TO STATE CHAMPIONSHIP HIGH SCHOOL RODEO ARENA
HALLETTSVILLE, TEX.

This view of the front of the entrance to the rodeo grounds is where the State Championship High School Rodeo was held in Hallettsville.

Grafe's Place, owned by Victor Grafe, was located on the east side of the square, fronting La Grange Street. The business had its beginning in 1937 as Grafe's Creamery on Third Street adjoining Eissler Bakery. The business was sold in 1970.

As student enrollment expanded, Sacred Heart School needed new facilities. Ground-breaking ceremonies were held in 1949, and in 1950, the new Sacred Heart School and Convent was completed at a cost of $220,000. The new campus faced Texana Street.

The Renger Memorial Hospital, named in memory of Dr. Paul Renger, was built and opened to the public in April 1950. It had a 30-bed capacity and boasted a modern baby-delivery room and one of the finest surgery rooms in the country.

Triangle Motel
Intersection of Highways U. S. 90-A, U. S. 77 & U. S. 77-A
Hallettsville, Texas

The Triangle Motel was located at the highway triangle of Highways 90A, 77, and 77A on the west side of Hallettsville. The motel was built in the early 1950s.

This photograph from the early 1950s was taken facing north on Main Street and at the west side of the square. The First National Bank of Hallettsville is on the immediate left, with the city hall directly across the street.

A Lavaca County Farm Bureau float passes in front of the Ben Franklin five-and-dime store in 1953.

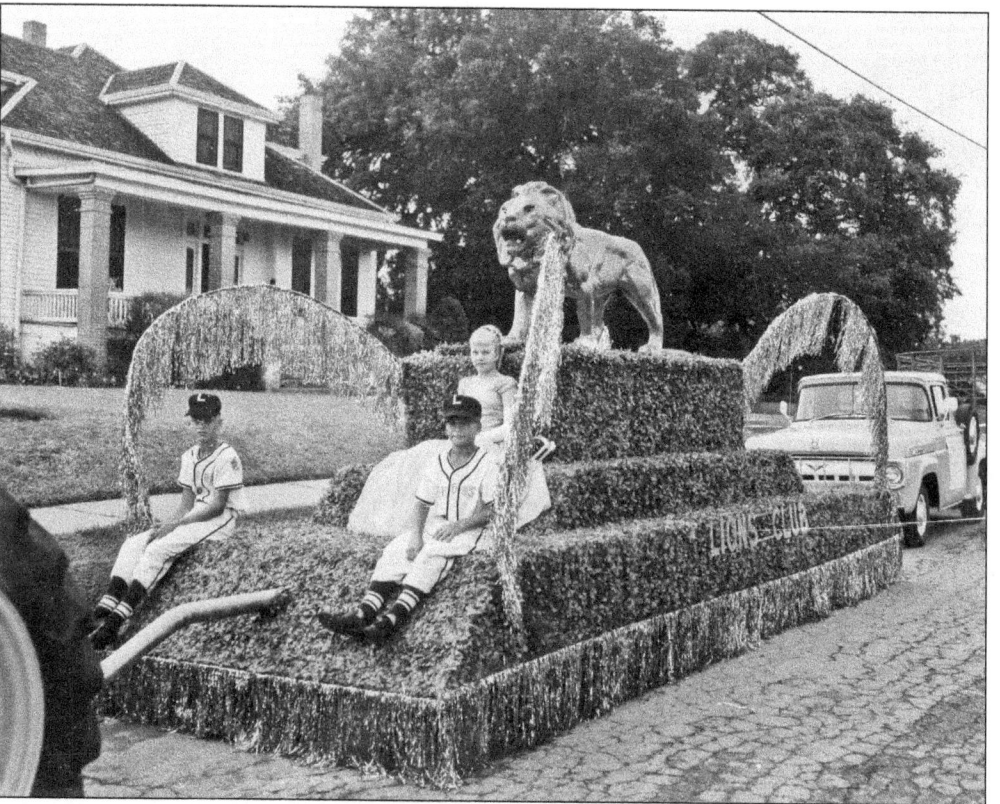

A Lions Club Little League float is pictured in a parade, passing in front of the former H.J. Heye residence, which is now the Lavaca County Historical Museum.

Pictured here is the Lone Star Beer wagon in the June Rodeo Parade as it passes Elkin's and the Ben Franklin five-and-dime store.

The Methodist Church in Hallettsville was established in 1851. The formal opening for the sanctuary was on January 25, 1953.

In 1954, the First National Bank began major reconstruction to double its interior space after obtaining the Louis Matula property next door. The vault pictured remained in service during the remodel, with money and records being moved in and out twice daily on a freight dolly with an armed escort.

The recreation hall, built in 1940, was a popular place for teen dances. The American Legion originally leased the hall from the city, but in 1963, it purchased the hall. This hall burnt to the ground in 1965.

Pictured here is Pam Taylor from Blanco, Texas, who was named the 1962 State Championship High School Rodeo Queen. In 1962, she also won the national sportsmanship award.

This is a view of the north side of the Lavaca County Courthouse Square anchored by the Meyerhoff Building on the northwest corner. The Meyerhoff Building was erected in 1909 to house Meyerhoff Dry Goods. The New York Store opened in this location in the mid-1950s.

Street Scene
Hallettsville, Texas

Bel Air Motel & Restaurant
Intersection Hi-Ways U. S. 90A and 77
Hallettsville, Texas

The Bel Air Motel opened for business on Sunday, July 21, 1957. The motel was located on the west side of Hallettsville at the triangle intersection of Highways 90A and 77A. It was owned and operated by Mr. and Mrs. Chester Allen.

Cloud 9 Motel
U. S. Hi-ways 77 & 90A
Hallettsville, Texas

The Cloud 9 Motel held its open house on Sunday, March 3, 1963. At the time of the open house, the motel had already been open to the public for several weeks. It is located at the intersection of Highways 90A and 77A. Mr. and Mrs. C.I. Fryer and Mr. and Mrs. J.J. Chott were the builders and operators, respectively.

Shown is the June 1957 Southwestern Bell Telephone Company phone directory cover for Hallettsville, Texas.

HALLETTSVILLE, TEXAS

TELEPHONE DIRECTORY

JUNE 1957

SEE PAGES 1 AND 2 FOR EMERGENCY CALLS
AND OTHER IMPORTANT INFORMATION

SEE THE "CLASSIFIED"
IN THIS DIRECTORY | 'YELLOW PAGES' | ITS YELLOW PAGES TELL
YOU "WHERE TO BUY IT"

SOUTHWESTERN BELL TELEPHONE COMPANY

COUNTY—ENGINES 5

Gindlers
DEPARTMENT STORE

Formerly Lauterstein's
LADIES & MEN'S READY-TO-WEAR
Nationally Advertised Brands

- Clausner Hosiery
- Seamprufe Lingerie
- Florsheim Shoes
- Arrow Shirts
- Stetson Hats
- Esquire Socks
- Children & Infants Wear
- Dry Goods
- Samsonite Luggage

Phone 175
South Side of Square
AIR CONDITIONED

This is a 1959 advertisement for Gindlers Department Store, formerly Lauterstein's. Located on the south side of the square, the store carried ladies' and men's ready-to-wear and nationally advertised brands and offered air conditioning. The phone number was 175.

John Rothabuer was the manager of the John F. Grant Lumber Company, which sold building materials and provided referrals to competent building contractors.

Tumis Service Station was located on 203 West Fourth Street. The business picked up and delivered cars for service.

The existing Hallettsville High School building opened on September 3, 1957. This structure is a remodel and expansion of the building that was originally erected in 1920.

This African American school opened in September 1957 and was located on land purchased from Louis Haidusek. The school was named Stevens–Mayo in honor of two prominent black educators: P.S. Stevens and J.E. Mayo. The school was dedicated on March 16, 1958.

Pictured is the aftermath of a traffic accident at the busy intersection of Main and Fourth Streets. Magnolia Mobile gas station is in the background along with the Heye-Zaruba car dealership.

The jail, seen here, was built in 1885. It was designed by J.E. Dietz and built by Pickett and Mead for $12,111.

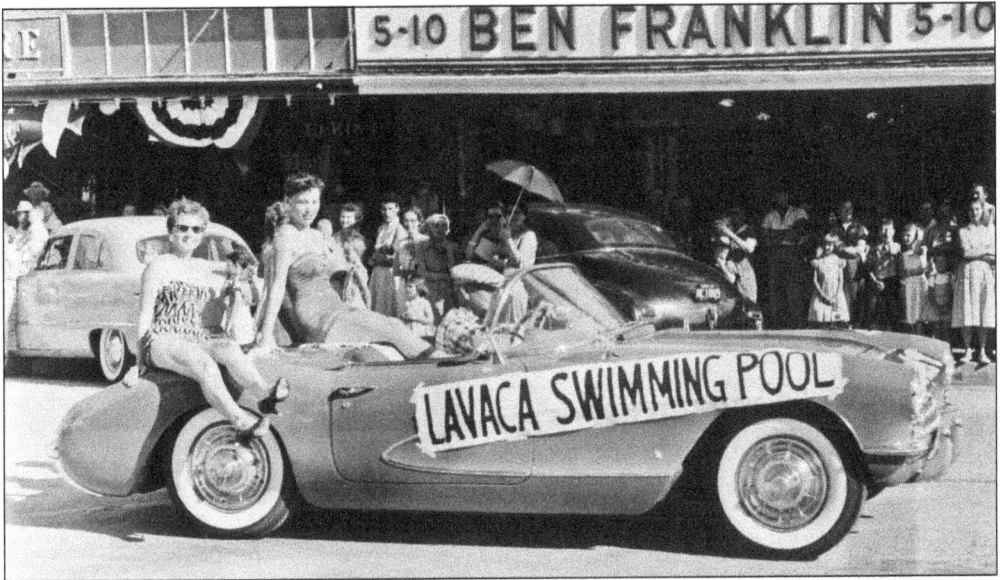

The Lavaca Swimming Pool float with Frances Dolezal and Gaynell Schroeder is seen here in 1958.

Shown is a program cover from the State Championship High School Rodeo, hosted by Hallettsville from June 17 to 20 in 1959.

A Hallettsville Chamber of Commerce float in the June 1959 Texas State High School Rodeo parade is pictured here.

This is a view of tomatoes being delivered by local farmers along the railroad tracks. The tomatoes were moved by railroad from Hallettsville to outside markets. The Hallettsville Train Depot is located in the bottom-right corner of the photograph.

Pictured here is the courthouse as it appeared sometime in the 1960s. Looking from the southwest, one can see that the trees and shrubs are taking over the courthouse lawn, crowding the building. The Confederate marker is barely visible beneath the tree in the foreground. But after more than 60 years, the courthouse is still viewed as "Grand, Complete & Perfect," as described by author Doug Kubicek.

This funnel-shaped cloud first touched down at Breslau and destroyed the Lavaca Courts Motel, a tourist lodge, and a café along the Hallettsville–Schulenburg Highway. Estimated damages at the time of the storm were more than $100,000. The storm occurred around 1:15 p.m. on October 18, 1960.

Shown here is the damage the tornado caused in Lavaca and Fayette Counties. This photograph is of the Lavaca Courts Motel on Highway 77 North that was destroyed by the tornado in October 1960.

This is a photograph of a home and business on Highway 77 North after the 1960 tornado.

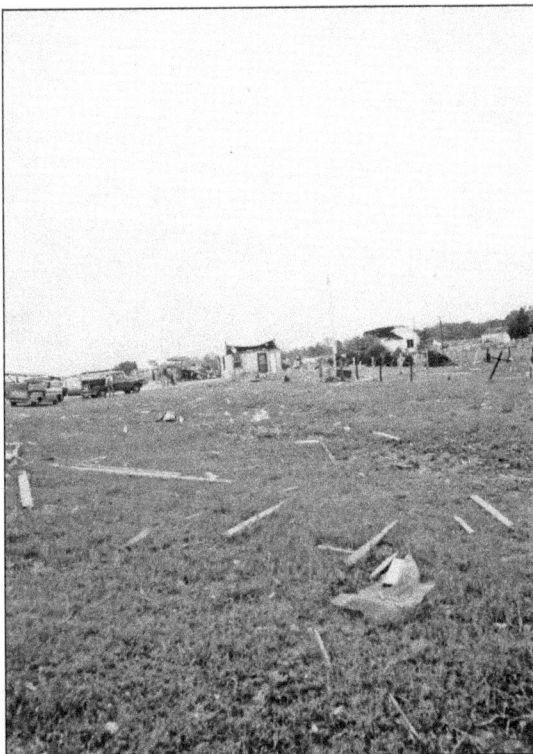

This is another view of the debris from the Lavaca Courts Motel on Highway 77 North after the tornado struck.

This view of a wrecked building is from tornado damage in 1960. About a dozen men are looking at the debris.

Seen here is the home of James H. Simpson, cashier at the First National Bank. The Simpson house, chosen for "yard of the month" in the early 1960s, was located on East Third Street. The house is of Spanish Colonial design.

Pictured is Bernice Jones of Hallettsville on horseback. Jones was All-Around Champion High School Cowgirl of Texas at the State Championship High School Rodeo, held at the Hallettsville Rodeo Arena in 1960.

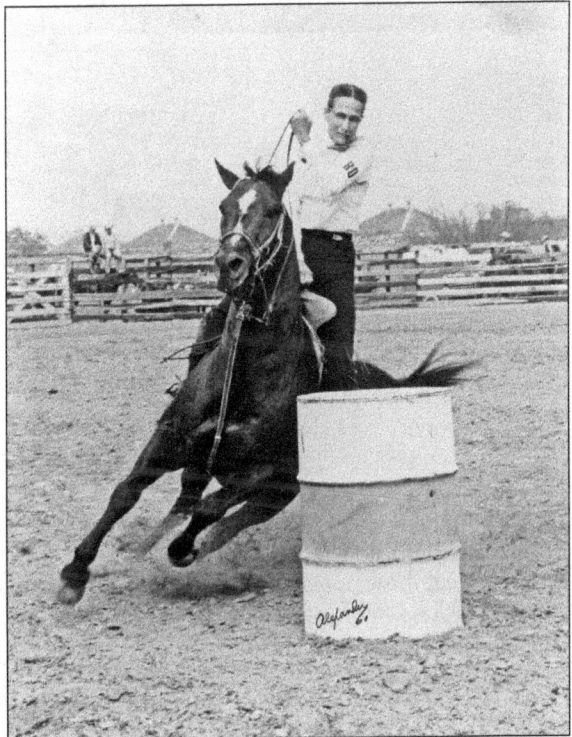

Gladys Menking participates in barrel racing, riding a horse called Speckles in 1961 at the rodeo in Hallettsville.

Dorothy St. Clair, from Yoakum, Texas, was selected as the 1961–1962 queen of the State Championship High School Rodeo. The first annual Texas State Championship High School Rodeo was held in 1947 in Hallettsville.

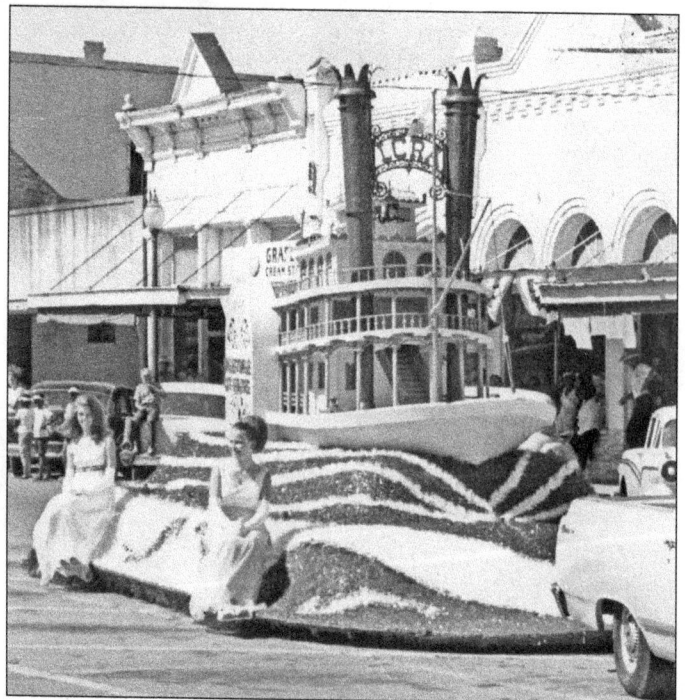

This is the Lower Colorado River Authority Parade float of a steamboat from the early 1960s. Gail Buske and Sandra King sit on the float. Grafe's Creamery can be seen in the background just to the left of the float.

The 1963 San Antonio Rodeo float is seen on the east side of the square in Hallettsville. The Fred Melnar Cafe and Bar was located on the corner of La Grange and Second Streets with the I. Samusch Building next to it.

Shown is a Goedecke Giants team photograph. Otto Goedecke, a cotton merchant and local businessman, sponsored this Little League team as part of his many civic interests. Goedecke was also a member of the Hallettsville Rotary Club.

The American Legion purchased the original recreation hall built in 1940 from the city in 1963. A fire destroyed the hall in 1965, and a new hall was constructed and opened to the public in December 1965. The hall is located at 107 East Park Street.

Henri Mae Jones, daughter of Mr. and Mrs. Burnett Jones of Hallettsville was crowned 1965 Yoakum Tom-Tom Rodeo Queen. In this photograph, she holds her trophy from the rodeo.

After playing defensive tackle for Texas Southern, Andy Rice, born in Hallettsville in 1940, won the AFL Championship in 1966 with the Kansas City Chiefs and played in the first AFL-NFL World Championship Game. The following year, he played for the Houston Oilers and Cincinnati Bengals.

The 1966 Hallettsville Chamber of Commerce Rodeo Queen, Glenda Zappe, rides the Hallettsville Chamber of Commerce and Agriculture float promoting the June state rodeo. Zappe is the daughter of Mr. and Mrs. Otto Lee Zappe of Hallettsville, Texas.

This view, taken from the courthouse, faces toward First and North Main Streets. The county jail is in the center.

A group of local dignitaries, including Hallettsville mayor Robert Kubena (left), First National Bank president J.H. Simpson Jr., and Hallettsville Chamber of Commerce secretary Mildred O'Brien, display a promotional bumper sticker for Hallettsville, "City of Hospitality."

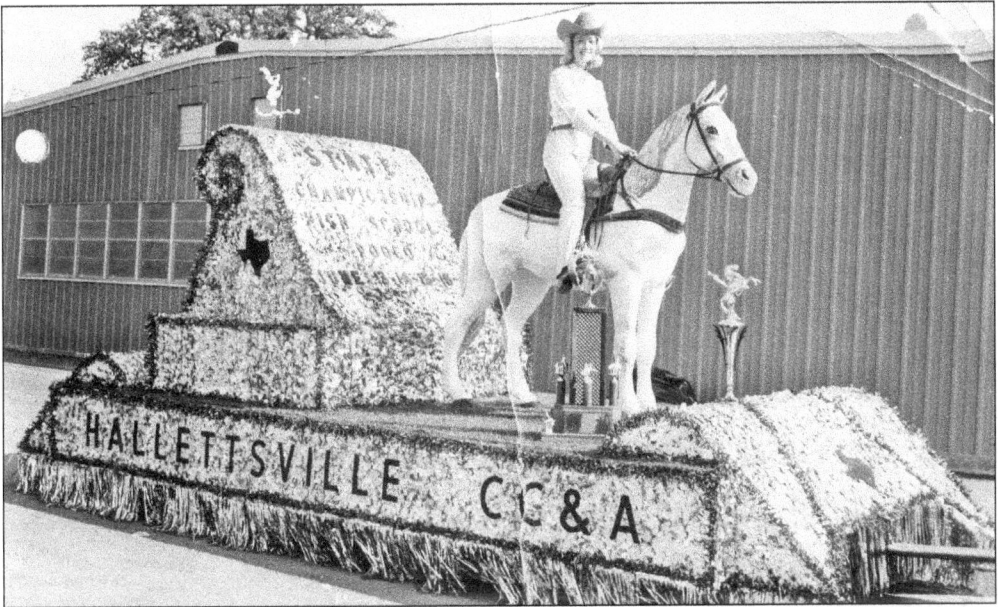

Rusty Lynn Miller, daughter of Mr. and Mrs. Russell Miller of Hallettsville, was crowned Queen of the Yoakum Tom-Tom Rodeo in 1964. She is seen here on the Hallettsville Chamber of Commerce and Agriculture parade float advertising the State Championship High School Rodeo in 1967.

The Hallettsville High School Twirlers pose in front of the "Hanging Tree," located next to the clubhouse of the Hallettsville Golf Association. An Indian named Pocket was hung on these gallows on September 12, 1879, for killing an Englishman named Leonard Hyde. The Hanging Tree received a historical marker in 1967.

Hallettsville Chamber of Commerce and Agriculture Rodeo Queen Susan Dolezal rides the chamber's parade float advertising the State Championship High School Rodeo in 1968.

Items produced by Janak Packing Co. are on display at the 1969 Hallettsville Chamber of Commerce banquet. The theme of the banquet was "Honoring Local Industry." Displays from various local industries showcased products being manufactured or produced in Hallettsville.

People gathered in front of the First National Bank in Hallettsville on November 20, 1969. The event was the dedication of the Texas Historical Marker, which had been placed on the bank building.

Here is a clearer view of the First National Bank of Hallettsville following the official Texas Historical Marker dedication in November 1969.

This night scene is of the opening ceremonies of the State Championship High School Rodeo held in Hallettsville.

Pictured are members of the Hallettsville High School class of 1930 at their class reunion on June 28, 1975. The photograph was taken at the Bel Air Restaurant. Former superintendent and Lavaca County judge Paul C. Boethel was a guest speaker at this 45-year class reunion.

Seen here are individuals who received plaques at the 1975 rodeo events held in Hallettsville, Texas. The rodeo brought many participants from other states, including California, Kansas, New Mexico, and North Dakota.

Spectators stand and sit outside Kahanek & Renger Drug Store, watching a parade on the Hallettsville square about 1976.

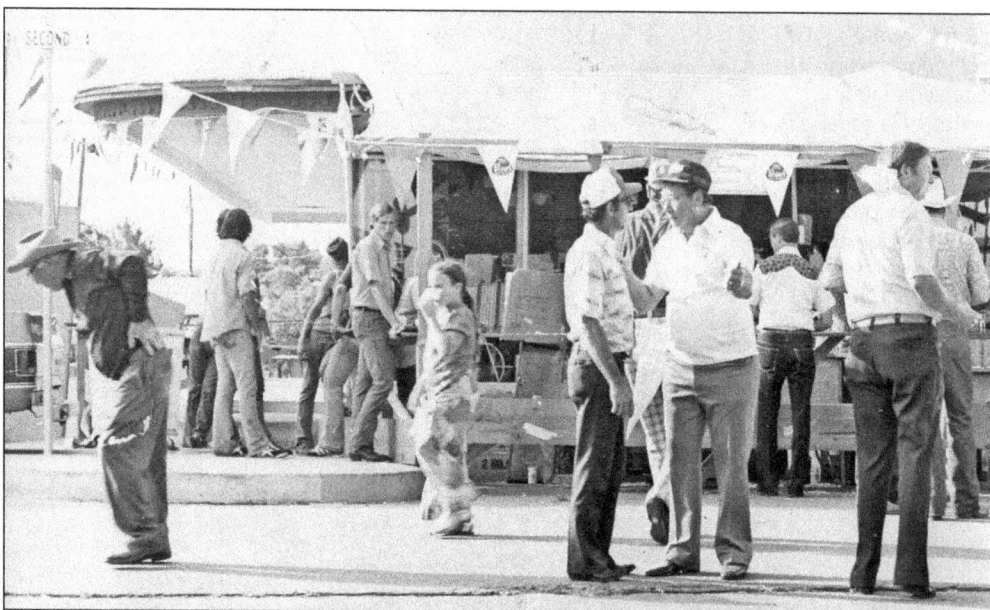

More parade spectators enjoy the street vendors at the corner of Second and Main Streets in front of Grahmann's True Value store.

At the heart of the action is the state high school championship rodeo announcer's booth. In the booth are, from left to right, Charlie Geisber (rodeo announcer), Peggy (Skelton) Kubicek, Paul Cook, and Virginia Smith (timekeeper).

The Ben Franklin store resides in the original H.J. Heye Building on the south side of the square as seen from the courthouse. The Court House Square Floral and Gifts is next door to the left.

In this view looking south from the courthouse toward Highway 77, the fire station is in the center of the image, and Mr. Gatti's is next door; it is currently home of the Hallettsville Police Department.

This is an aerial photograph taken of Hallettsville and its courthouse, looking northwest. Sacred Heart Church and School are seen in the foreground, and the two-story jail is visible to the right of the courthouse.

The First National Bank, located on the corner of West Third and South Main Streets, is pictured here.

Seen here is Ehler's Furniture and Appliance in Hallettsville's business district on the corner of Third and North Texana Streets (Highway 77 North).

116

This is a view of the Renger Bar during the August 1981 flood. Grahmann's True Value Hardware can be seen on the far right of the photograph.

Notches in the doorway of the Lavaca County Courthouse building show how high the water reached during the 1940 and 1981 floods.

Water floods the square in
1981. The courthouse is
on the left, the bandstand
is in the center, and
Ehler's is on the right.

Rains from a tropical depression in 1981 caused a flood, which inundated the jail, leaving only the second floor untouched.

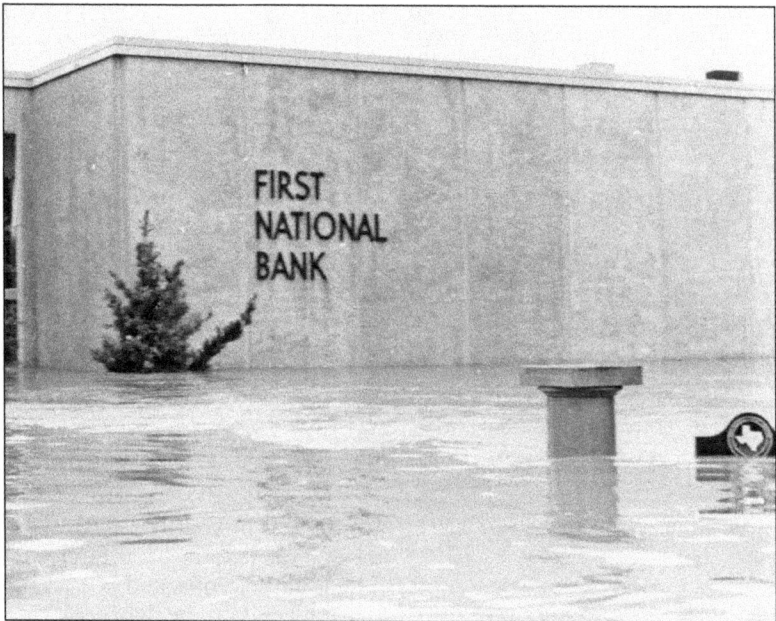

This is a view of the First National Bank during the 1981 flood. Notice the historical marker on the right, the top just barely poking above the floodwaters.

Pictured is an aerial view of Ludwig's Repair shop with the Lavaca River in the foreground. Beyond it is the Hallettsville bridge (center), and Hoffer's gas station is the large building to the left in 1981.

The floodwaters of August 31, 1981, surround the Lavaca County Jail.

Above is a 1985 group photograph of the Hallettsville Volunteer Fire Department members in front of the courthouse. Included in the image are their firefighting vehicles.

Hallettsville Fire Department - 1986

Seen here is the Hallettsville Volunteer Fire Department of 1986. Pictured from left to right in the front row are Chief Roy Kalisek, first assistant chief John D. Henneke, second assistant chief Harold Ludwig, Pres. Alvin Paul Grahmann, Vice Pres. Erwin Holly, treasurer Frank Luke, secretary Forrest W. Timm Jr., and drillmaster Anthony Ludwig.

The picture is of the Hallettsville Reading Club in 1986. Some members included Tavali Mullins, Mary Treptow, Lillian Deavers, Hazel Timm, Eileen Lindemann, and Beulah Wilson. The club supported the Frienrch Simpson Memorial Library by volunteering for book sales.

William O. "Bill" Renger (1918– 2002) stands in front of the Renger Bar on the northwest corner of the Lavaca County Courthouse Square in Hallettsville. Renger operated the bar from 1955 to 1998. The building was designed by James Riely Gordon.

This is an inside view of the altar of the St. James Episcopal Church. St. James Episcopal is a mission church working with other area Episcopal churches. In 1995, St. James established partnerships with seven other area congregations to provide a support network.

The Lavaca Historical Museum, founded in 1990, is housed in what was originally the home of H.J. Heye, owner of the Heye Saddlery and Harness. The second floor was added in around 1900. The museum moved from here in the fall of 2012 to its new building on Highway 77 North.

The courthouse has been lit up at Christmas ever since World War II. In 1996, a group of citizens began the festival of lights the weekend after Thanksgiving, celebrating the town's past and present so locals can catch a glimpse of the future of peace, envision hope, celebrate joy, and share the love of Christmas.

BIBLIOGRAPHY

125th Anniversary Book Committee. *Sacred Heart Church & Catholic School, Hallettsville, Texas, 1882–2007, 125th Anniversary.* Hallettsville, TX: Sacred Heart Catholic Church, 2007.

Boethel, Paul C. *History of Lavaca County.* Austin, TX: Von Boeckmann-Jones, 1959.

Boethel, Paul C. *Lavaca County Seats And Their Courthouses.* Hallettsville, TX: The Lavaca County Historical Commission, 1997.

Centennial Book Committee. *Sacred Heart Parish, A Century of Service for God & Country, 1882-1982.* Hallettsville, TX: Sacred Heart Catholic Church, 1982.

Friench Simpson Memorial Library, Vertical Family Name Files and Newspapers, Hallettsville, TX: Friench Simpson Memorial Holdings, 1846–2010.

Kubicek, Doug. *Grand, Complete & Perfect: The Lavaca County Courthouse.* Hallettsville, TX: The Old Homestead Publishing Company, 1997.

Meyers, David and Pat. *Marking History in Lavaca County.* Hallettsville, TX: Lavaca County Historical Commission and The Raymond Dickson Foundation, 2001.

Rhodes, Anne and Fishcar Frank. *Hallettsville And Its Volunteer Fire Department.* Schulenburg, TX: Schulenburg Printing and Office Supplies, Inc., 2003.

Sacred Heart Parish Staff. *Souvenir of Diamond Jubilee of Sacred Heart Church, Parish and Rectory, Convent and School, Hallettsville, Texas 1882–1957.* Hallettsville, TX: Sacred Heart Catholic Church, 1957.

Simpson, James H. Jr. *A Century In Hallettsville: The History of First National Bank 1888–1988.* Hallettsville, TX: First National Bank, 1988.

ABOUT THE ORGANIZATION

The Lavaca County Record Retention Volunteers, also known as "the Press Gang," consists of a group of individuals who have committed time and money to the preservation and protection of the historical documents of Lavaca County, Texas. The nickname refers to the days when pirates would "impress" or basically hijack people into service. The record retention movement in Lavaca County began in May 2004, and over the past eight years, the volunteers have hand-cleaned, rehoused, inventoried, and scanned thousands of pages of documents that chronicle the development of Lavaca County and its citizens, past, present, and future. The group has worked closely with and been mentored by Rebecca Elder, an adjunct preservation field services officer for Amigos Library Services, and Elizabeth Kouba, the county clerk and records management official for Lavaca County, Texas.

Visit us at
arcadiapublishing.com